Endorsements for the Church Questions Series

"Christians are pressed by very real questions. How does Scripture structure a church, order worship, organize ministry, and define biblical leadership? Those are just examples of the questions that are answered clearly, carefully, and winsomely in this new series from 9Marks. I am so thankful for this ministry and for its incredibly healthy and hopeful influence in so many faithful churches. I eagerly commend this series."

R. Albert Mohler Jr., President, The Southern Baptist Theological Seminary

"Sincere questions deserve thoughtful answers. If you're not sure where to start in answering these questions, let this series serve as a diving board into the pool. These minibooks are winsomely to-the-point and great to read together with one friend or one hundred friends."

Gloria Furman, author, *Missional Motherhood* and *The Pastor's Wife*

"As a pastor, I get asked lots of questions. I'm approached by unbelievers seeking to understand the gospel, new believers unsure about next steps, and maturing believers wanting help answering questions from their Christian family, friends, neighbors, or coworkers. It's in these moments that I wish I had a book to give them that was brief, answered their questions, and pointed them in the right direction for further study. Church Questions is a series that provides just that. Each booklet tackles one question in a biblical, brief, and practical manner. The series may be called Church Questions, but it could be called 'Church Answers.' I intend to pick these up by the dozens and give them away regularly. You should too."

Juan R. Sanchez, Senior Pastor, High Pointe Baptist Church, Austin, Texas

"Where can we Christians find reliable answers to our common questions about life together at church—without having to plow through long, expensive books? The Church Questions booklets meet our need with answers that are biblical, thoughtful, and practical. For pastors, this series will prove a trustworthy resource for guiding church members toward deeper wisdom and stronger unity."

Ray Ortlund, President, Renewal Ministries

How Can I Make the Most of Sunday Services?

Church Questions

Can Women Be Pastors?, Greg Gilbert
Does It Matter What I Believe?, Samuel James
Does the Gospel Promise Health and Prosperity?, Sean DeMars
Does the Old Testament Really Point to Jesus?, David M. King
How Can I Be Sure I'm Saved?, Jeremy Pierre
How Can I Begin to Teach the Bible?, David Helm
How Can I Encourage My Pastors?, Carmyn Zamora
How Can I Get More Out of My Bible Reading?, Jeremy Kimble
How Can I Grow in Hospitality?, Keri Folmar
How Can I Love Church Members with Different Politics?, Jonathan Leeman and Andy Naselli
How Can I Make the Most of Sunday Services?, Erin Wheeler
How Can I Serve My Church?, Matthew Emadi
How Can Women Thrive in the Local Church?, Keri Folmar
How Do I Disciple Others?, J. Garret Kell
How Do I Fight Sin and Temptation?, J. Garret Kell
How Do I Get Started in Evangelism?, Mack Stiles
Is God Really Sovereign?, Conrad Mbewe
Is Hell Real?, Dane Ortlund
Should I Be a Missionary?, Andy Johnson
What Do Deacons Do?, Juan Sanchez
What If I'm Discouraged in My Evangelism?, Isaac Adams
What If I've been Hurt by My Church?, Daniel P. Miller
What Is a Church?, Matthew Emadi
What Is the Church's Mission?, Jonathan Leeman
What Should I Do Now That I'm a Christian?, Sam Emadi
What Should I Look for in a Church?, Alex Duke
Who's in Charge of the Church?, Sam Emadi
Why Should I Be Baptized?, Bobby Jamieson
Why Should I Give to My Church?, Jamie Dunlop
Why Should I Join a Church?, Mark Dever

How Can I Make the Most of Sunday Services?

Erin Wheeler

WHEATON, ILLINOIS

How Can I Make the Most of Sunday Services?

© 2025 by 9Marks

Published by Crossway
    1300 Crescent Street
    Wheaton, Illinois 60187

All rights reserved. No part of this publication may be reproduced, stored in a retrieval system, or transmitted in any form by any means, electronic, mechanical, photocopy, recording, or otherwise, without the prior permission of the publisher, except as provided for by USA copyright law. Crossway® is a registered trademark in the United States of America.

Cover image and design: Jordan Singer

First printing 2025

Printed in the United States of America

Scripture quotations are from the ESV® Bible (The Holy Bible, English Standard Version®), © 2001 by Crossway, a publishing ministry of Good News Publishers. Used by permission. All rights reserved. The ESV text may not be quoted in any publication made available to the public by a Creative Commons license. The ESV may not be translated in whole or in part into any other language.

All emphases in Scripture quotations have been added by the author.

Trade paperback ISBN: 978-1-4335-9150-1
ePub ISBN: 978-1-4335-9152-5
PDF ISBN: 978-1-4335-9151-8

Library of Congress Cataloging-in-Publication Data

Names: Wheeler, Erin, author.
Title: How can I make the most of Sunday services? / Erin Wheeler.
Description: Wheaton, Illinois : Crossway, 2025. | Series: Church questions | Includes bibliographical references and index.
Identifiers: LCCN 2024018889 (print) | LCCN 2024018890 (ebook) | ISBN 9781433591501 (trade paperback) | ISBN 9781433591518 (pdf) | ISBN 9781433591525 (epub)
Subjects: LCSH: Public worship. | Lord's Supper. | Church attendance.
Classification: LCC BV5 .W45 2025 (print) | LCC BV5 (ebook) | DDC 264—dc23/eng/20240711
LC record available at https://lccn.loc.gov/2024018889
LC ebook record available at https://lccn.loc.gov/2024018890

Crossway is a publishing ministry of Good News Publishers.

BP		34	33	32	31	30	29	28	27	26	25
15	14	13	12	11	10	9	8	7	6	5	4	3	2	1

For a day in your courts is better
> than a thousand elsewhere.
I would rather be a doorkeeper in the
> house of my God
> > than dwell in the tents of wickedness.

Psalm 84:10

Growing up, my Sunday mornings typically began by watching my parents figure out which service our family would attend. Once they decided, my siblings and I, bleary-eyed from waking up late, raced each other to the car. I'd scramble into the vehicle with wet hair from the shower I managed to squeeze in 10 minutes before. Once we arrived, I sang along quietly while the praise band belted their original tunes—they seemed to have a new song every week. I'd listen to the sermon while also wondering what we were going to eat for lunch—after all, I'd clearly gotten up too late for breakfast.

After marrying my husband Brad, we began looking for a new church. What were we looking for? We knew we wanted the word of God to be central, but we really didn't know what that should look like. We also wanted a certain "feeling" in the service but didn't know how to put that particular conviction into words.

We eventually landed in a pew at a church in Washington, DC. If we were going for a "feeling," this place didn't have it. I stumbled my way through old hymns, creeds, and antiphonal Scripture readings. It was the furthest thing from my casual California church upbringing. I felt out-of-place and confused—and yet, something drew us back week after week. Every part of the service had a purpose. Evident joy filled the room as the congregation loudly sang each song. The people clearly revered God's word, and they hung around for what seemed like forever after the service ended, talking about the sermon, praying for each other, confessing sin, and sharing struggles.

But what caught our attention most was what was happening inside us. We were growing like we never had before.

How Can I Make the Most of Sunday Services?

We joined the church and began to understand what the Bible says about God's design for the local church. We grew more excited about gathering with our church family each week, seeking to make the most of our Sunday mornings together. Over time, we began to see the importance of participating and serving, not just observing and consuming.

What about you? How do you think about the local church, particularly its corporate worship? Are you confused about what happens in your church? Are you bored? Do you feel like you're not getting much out of the service? Do you know what God's word says should be prioritized when the church gathers? Maybe your church has gone through some changes and you wish things could just go back to the way things were!

Read on, friend, this booklet is for you.

My hope is that in the following pages you'll see how God has designed corporate worship, why it matters for your spiritual health, and how you can make the most out of Sunday services.

But before we get there, we need to learn a fundamental lesson: corporate worship is just not about you.

It's Just Not about You

I work as a nurse. At our monthly staff meeting, we review our hospital's vision statement. It can feel rote, but it actually reminds us how each employee contributes to the larger goal. Vision statements keep first things first. If you know *why* you're doing what you're doing, then you're better equipped to choose the right actions to meet that goal.

The Bible gives local churches a "vision" for what they should prioritize, particularly in corporate worship. Unfortunately, too many Christians develop their own personal vision statements and then impose them on the local church. We think the church exists to cater to our preferences or to give us a certain "feeling" or "experience" of worship. But corporate worship isn't meant to cater to our desires.

It's just not about us.

How Can I Make the Most of Sunday Services?

Our church's gatherings are ultimately about God. We worship according to his desires, not ours. When we gather we should be governed by God's word, not our preferences.

The Bible indicates that there are two ways you can commit the sin of idolatry. The first way is to worship something other than God: Molech, Marduk, a statue, your beauty, money, success, a happy family, or any other thing, good or bad, that's not God. The second way to commit idolatry—one we regrettably give far less attention to—is to worship God the wrong way. Many Christians are careful to avoid the first path to idolatry but are often unaware of this second path.

As a result, we let entertainment culture, tradition, or personal preferences dictate what we do in church. But orchestrating our corporate worship around tradition, what we "like," or what makes us "feel" close to God isn't just unfaithful, it's self-destructive. It's like a little kid who pulls a stool up to the stove, turns the range on high heat, and proceeds to throw a Cadbury candy creme egg into the pan in an attempt to make scrambled eggs according to his way and by "hisself." It's just plain foolish, not to mention dangerous and messy!

So the first thing you need to do to make the most of the Sunday service is recognize that it isn't about you. It's about worshiping God in the way he commands and according to his desires. We'll talk more about what that looks like a bit later. But for now, let's just get this point down. Corporate worship isn't about having a souped-up quiet time in the company of other Christians. It's about gathering with God's people, checking our preferences at the door, and worshiping the one true God in the way he commands.

Corporate Worship, Not Entertainment Weekly

We can make the most of corporate worship if we understand why we're there in the first place. And praise God, he hasn't left us alone to figure it out!

Scripture repeatedly shows us that God assembles his people for the express purpose of exalting him and edifying one another. Before the coming of Christ, Israel—God's people under the Old Covenant—gathered at the tent of meeting (Ex. 40:34) or the tabernacle in the wilderness (Num. 9:15) to worship him. They assembled to worship at the temple (1 Kings 8:1–11). They also assembled to praise God for the rebuilding of the walls of Jerusalem (Ezra 3:10–13). They listened to God's word being publicly read (Luke 4:16). In the new covenant, the church continued this pattern of gathering to worship God corporately. They assembled together in local churches to devote themselves to the apostles' teaching, to pray, to sing, and to celebrate the Lord's Supper (Acts 2:42–47). God has always gathered his people so that they would exalt him *together*.

Why does God gather his people to worship him? Consider these two reasons.

1. We Gather to Edify

First, gathering encourages and edifies the saints. When we're together doing what God has called us to do, we build one another up in our most holy faith (Jude 20).

When God saves us, he saves us into the church—the family of God. Like a family, each person contributes to the welfare of the home. The same is true for the church. As members of the same family, we gather each week to help one another and contribute to the well-being of the church. Yet many view corporate worship as consumers, not providers. But when the Bible talks about the church, it doesn't talk about "me" and "them" but about "us." The church is an "us"—a family gathered to worship and serve.

As Paul taught, the church is one body with many parts (1 Cor. 12:20). You might have a more public role or you might serve in quiet, unseen ways like making coffee or restocking the bathroom paper towels. Or you might simply serve by a faithful ministry of presence, singing gospel songs to those around you, praying for a brother or sister after the service, or encouraging others by being an attentive listener to God's word.

How Can I Make the Most of Sunday Services?

Corporate worship is never a spectator sport. We gather to worship God and encourage one another—and that takes work. We don't simply "attend" church in the same way we "attend" a concert or a baseball game. We *are* the church, and each one of us has a role to play! We honor and exalt the Lord Jesus when we come to corporate worship ready to serve others.

A good friend in our church suffers with a chronic illness. She often can't make it to corporate worship. But when she's able to come, her physical presence fills the room. She praises the Lord with her fragile hands turned up to God, sitting in her seat with a look of joy on her face. Seeing her faith and perseverance year after year strengthens our whole congregation. She edifies us all just by her presence.

Your faithful attendance and service does the same. As fellow members consider your life, your afflictions, your joys, and your obedience to Jesus, they're edified by your ministry of presence. They're encouraged by hearing you sing. They're heartened by having a conversation with you after the service. We can't edify one another if we never see each other.

We gather to edify.

2. We Gather to Evangelize

Second, gathering with the saints for worship *indirectly* acts as a means of evangelism. The apostle Paul makes this point in 1 Corinthians 14:24–25, saying that if "an unbeliever or outsider enters, he is convicted by all, he is called to account by all, the secrets of his heart are disclosed, and so, falling on his face, he will worship God and declare that God is really among you."

Corporate worship isn't designed for unbelievers—the primary purpose is to edify the saints. At the same time, an unbeliever might show up. We hope they do! And when they do, Paul says they should recognize through the church's corporate worship that God is really among us! Corporate worship pulls back the curtain and gives unbelievers a backstage pass to the life of the church. They get to see what the Christian life is about: exalting God, celebrating the good news of the gospel, and edifying one another.

Directions for Assembly

If you've ever purchased a piece of furniture from IKEA, you know the agonizing experience of trying to assemble it. Nothing taxes a friendship (or a marriage!) more. Both people have an idea of what the end product should look like. But getting from pieces in a box to a finished product can be quite a feat.

Why did they give us eighteen extra screws? I think we're missing six nails. We don't have enough slats of wood. Why did they design the front and back pieces to look exactly the same!

Worst of all, IKEA instructions often contain no words—only blurry, obscure pictures. Sometimes it feels impossible to know which parts go where. I've been guilty of just assembling the pieces in whatever way I think best.

Christians sometimes approach the weekly gathering like this. In God's word, they don't see more than obscure pictures that allow us to configure corporate worship in whatever way we think best. But if we look carefully, we'll discover that God's word doesn't just give us a few obscure directions. In fact, God has designed corporate worship and given us explicit instructions for what the church should do. If we understand that worship has been designed by God, and if we know what he requires of us when we gather, then we'll know better how to prepare for that work.

God Designs Corporate Worship

God is the master designer of corporate worship. As one scholar noted, "God's glory *draws* our worship, and God's will *directs* our worship."[1]

God has explicitly commanded us how to worship him in his word. Pastors and theologians refer to this idea as the *regulative principle*. In short, God *regulates* how we should approach him in worship. We don't get to make it up as we go along. As one scholar helpfully points out,

> The key benefit of the regulative principle is that it helps to assure that God—not

man—is the supreme authority for how corporate worship should be conducted, by assuring that the Bible . . . is the prime factor in our conduct of and approach to corporate worship.[2]

Now you might read the phrase "regulative principle" and break out into an obligatory yawn. Or maybe you recoil because it sounds so restrictive. But for centuries, millions of Christians have recognized that strictly adhering to elements of worship commanded by God is *liberating*! Imagine going to church and being forced to participate in acts of worship that made you uncomfortable—or, worse, that you thought were unbiblical. Many Christians in the history of the church have found themselves subject to man-made inventions and innovations. How tremendously liberating, then, to attend a church committed to worshiping God only in ways he has required. By following God's instructions, we experience true freedom.

Scripture regularly warns us against worshiping according to our own ways. Nadab and Abihu believed they could offer "strange fire" that the Lord had never commanded. For this misstep, they were consumed by fire (Lev. 10:1–2). Saul offered an unauthorized sacrifice and had his kingdom stripped from him (1 Sam. 13:8–14). Uzzah transported the Ark of the Covenant on an oxcart instead of carrying it on poles as the Lord commanded. When he touched the ark, trying to save it from slipping into the mud, he was not commended for his piety but killed for his disobedience (2 Sam. 6:3–7).

Or consider the Pharisees, who broke the commandments of God for the sake of their tradition (Matt 15:3). Hitting even closer to home, consider the church at Corinth. Paul said in 1 Corinthians 11:27–30 that God judged the Corinthians with sickness and even death because they celebrated the Lord's Supper in ways that dishonored God.[3] Jesus taught that his disciples should worship God in both spirit *and* truth (John 4:23–24). The writer of Hebrews warns us saying, "Let us offer to God *acceptable* worship, with reverence and awe, for our God is a consuming fire" (Heb. 12:28–29).

These warnings are particularly important for Christians who live in a culture that celebrates novelty, creativity, innovation, and individuality. We would do well to heed the humorous remarks of C. S. Lewis:

> Novelty may fix our attention not even on the service but on the celebrant. You know what I mean. Try as one may to exclude it, the question "What on earth is he up to now?" will intrude. It lays one's devotion waste. There is really some excuse for the man who said, "I wish they'd remember that the charge to Peter was Feed my sheep; not Try experiments on my rats!"[4]

Essentials and Expressions

Does the regulative principle mean that every church needs to look exactly the same?

Not quite. The *essentials* for worship do not change, but the *expression* or *forms* of them can vary. Confused? Let me teach you some words theologians have used to explain how the regulative principle works out in real life. When you're thinking about a church's worship you have to learn to distinguish between elements and forms.

The *elements* of worship are the specific things God prescribes for corporate worship. They are the necessary ingredients: (1) preach the word, (2) pray the word, (3) read the word, (4) sing the word, and (5) see the word (baptism and the Lord's Supper are visual pictures of the word of the gospel).

The *forms* are the *expressions* of those elements. At this point, churches will differ from one another. For instance, one church might preach 30-minute sermons, another might have 70-minute sermons. Some churches might sing with no instrumentation, others with minimal instrumentation, while still others might sing with an orchestra. Churches will differ in how they arrange the service, organizing the elements of worship in different sequences. Churches will differ in what songs they sing, which translation of the Bible they read, how frequently they practice the Lord's Supper, and so on. But as you can see, two churches can be equally committed to the same *elements* of worship but might express those elements in different *forms*.

So whatever forms your church uses, you need to be most concerned about engaging with the elements of worship. So let's consider now some of those non-negotiable elements of worship and how to prepare ourselves to profit from each one.

The Beauty of the Ordinary and Orderly

Our growth in the grace and knowledge of God comes through what Christians have often called the "ordinary means of grace." When the church gathers, we preach the word, pray the word, read the word, sing the word, and see the word made visible in the ordinances.

The centrality of God's word in corporate worship is evident from the first days of the church. When the early church gathered, they kept the word front-and-center, devoting themselves to the apostles' teaching (Acts 2:42). They gathered as a people of God to listen to the word being read and preached (Acts 20:27; 1 Tim.

4:13; 2 Tim. 4:2), to sing the word together (Col. 3:16), and to pray (Acts 2:42; 1 Tim. 2:8). And in all this ministry around the word, they did everything "decently and in order" (1 Cor. 14:40).

Churches shouldn't be any different today. Let's consider a few of these in a little more detail.

Reading and Preaching the Word

At the center of corporate worship is the word of God. God's word gathers and instructs God's people.

As such, the reading of God's word should be a regular part of our corporate worship. Even Jesus stood in the temple and read the word aloud (Luke 4:16–21). Paul commanded his protégé Timothy, the pastor of the church at Ephesus, to read Scripture publicly to the church: "Until I come, devote yourself to the public reading of Scripture, to exhortation, to teaching" (1 Tim. 4:13).

Paul's instructions show us that churches shouldn't simply read Scripture together; a pastor should teach it and exhort the congregation from it. In other words, churches don't just gather to hear God's word read, they also gather to hear God's word preached.

Faithful preaching involves looking at a passage of Scripture, explaining its meaning in context, and then applying it to Christians today. This practice is often called *expositional preaching*—preaching where the main point of the passage is the main point of the sermon applied to the hearts of the hearers.

Of course, topical preaching may be appropriate at some times and even necessary. But it shouldn't be the *main diet*. We should be able to walk away from the sermon knowing Scripture better not just equipped with five steps for how to handle our anger.

As the people of God, we are to be people of his word. In the book of Acts, the Bereans were praised as those who "received the word with all eagerness, examining the Scriptures daily" to see if Paul's preaching was sound (Acts 17:11). We need to model ourselves after these brothers and sisters, seeking to know and understand the word of God as it's preached. If you're looking for a church, the single most important thing to consider is whether or not the word of God is preached regularly and cherished in all aspects of church family life together, even in the singing![5]

If reading and preaching God's word is to be primary in our church gatherings, then it needs to play a primary role in how you prepare for corporate worship. One productive way to prepare for preaching is by reading and studying the passage beforehand. You can do this individually, with your family, or even with a brother or sister in the church. Like chicken that's tenderized and tastier after being marinated for days, our hearts are receptive and open to receive the preached word after meditating on it throughout the week.

Singing Together

One Sunday, as the church was singing, my husband leaned over to me and whispered, "I don't like this song very much." I chuckled. "Well, it's actually a favorite of mine. I sing it to myself when I'm discouraged. And, honey, we sang it at our wedding!" He laughed with mild embarrassment and said, "I'll definitely sing this one differently next time." He continued to sing with the congregation but now with a bit more joy in his voice.

Music is a funny thing. It whirls and dances around our hearts and minds, invoking all kinds of emotions and memories. Church music is no different, which is why churches often experience disunity over it. We think we know what's best for our church's music selection, volume, instrumentation, vocals, and more. Sometimes Christians air those opinions passionately, without regard for the church's unity.

Other times we let our preferences cause us to become dissatisfied, disillusioned, or discontent. I have a friend who purposely arrives late to church because he "can't stand the music." Maybe you don't come late, but you might love an excuse to "skip out on that song."

If that's you, remember you have a role to play in the gathered church. You are a participant, not a spectator! Paul reminds us that every part of the body plays a role (1 Cor. 12:12–31), even in the church's music.

Last summer, our family visited another church while traveling. As we navigated our way through the parking lot, we came through the foyer to the double theater doors. When we opened the second set of doors, the sound was so loud and the room was so dark I inadvertently screamed and jumped on my son! Thankfully, the music overwhelmed my scream, and my kids found the entire sequence hysterical.

That church treated church music like a production. The room had been set up like a movie theater. I'm sure the church didn't mean for this to happen, but I couldn't help but think the people saw themselves more like an audience than active participants. While I'm sure the service was well intentioned, it focused more on creating a "mood" than actually discipling the congregation to sing. But God's word is clear: we sing *to* one another and *to* God as *one body*. Singing is a corporate activity.

For instance, in Ephesians 5:18–20, Paul exhorts the church at Ephesus saying,

> Do not get drunk with wine, for that is debauchery, but be filled with the Spirit, addressing one another in psalms and hymns and spiritual songs, singing and making melody to the Lord with your heart, giving thanks always and for everything to God the Father in the name of our Lord Jesus Christ.

As one author said, "Singing is part of each member's ministry to the whole body. When you join a church, you join the choir."[6]

Whether you *feel* the music is too sparse, too loud, too slow, too repetitive, too old, or too "something else," remember that God has called his people to worship him together with one heart and voice (Rom. 15:6). This might mean we have to check our musical preferences at the door and focus more on encouraging brothers and sisters than having a musical style that pleases us.

How people sing differs around the world, of course, but the content should not. We should always sing the truths of God's word. Sometimes those words are joyful, sometimes they are filled with sorrow and lament as we look upon the world and long for the day of our King's return.[7] Remember, "Our singing anticipates something else—another time and another place. Our singing is not yet what it one day will be. It offers a foretaste of the day when all of God's family will gather around the throne."[8]

Corporate Prayer

I was having coffee with a dear older member of our church when she began complaining about the length of the corporate prayers: "He prayed for five whole minutes. I know because I've started timing. They are so long! How can anyone pay attention to someone praying for that long?" I know she's not alone.

We ended up having a fruitful conversation about the importance of corporate prayer and how we can learn from them each Sunday morning. As I pointed out, word-centered prayers align our thoughts with God's. It lifts up our "eyes to the hills" where our help comes from (Ps. 121:1–2). Furthermore, corporate prayer teaches us how to pray individually. By witnessing and participating in mature prayers modeled in corporate worship, we learn how to pray ourselves. So prepare yourself for the work of prayer by reminding yourself that corporate worship is a greenhouse meant to grow our dependence on God.

Practical Ways to Prepare for Corporate Worship

Prepare Your Life

My son is a competitive swimmer. He spends a ridiculous amount of time gearing up for big races and preparing to be in the best shape possible. What I find particularly admirable is how much he prepares for his practices! He makes sure he eats well the night before, he packs breakfast and his bags for the next day. He *attempts* to get to bed early so he has enough rest.

He's learned well the old adage, "If you fail to prepare, you prepare to fail."

As Christians, we're preparing for a big event too. We're preparing for the return of our Savior. But until that comes, we must also prepare for all the little battles we'll face on the way to heaven. Paul tells us in Ephesians 6 how we must prepare for the battles we face as we await the return of King Jesus. We must put on the whole armor of God so we can stand against the devil's schemes. One of the ways we can practically do this is by gathering with our church family (see Heb. 10:24–25)!

We can't roll into corporate worship harried and hurried and expect, with empty bellies and empty hearts, to glean a lot from the time. Sure, there are times and even seasons when life feels impossible, and it's perfectly fine to just keep our heads above water. Even in those seasons, we can be confident that our gentle and lowly shepherd bids us come and find rest for our souls (Matt. 11:28–30).

But let's face it, sometimes the burdens we bring with us to a Sunday morning service are

How Can I Make the Most of Sunday Services?

the product of our own lack of planning. We slide into our seats with our rears on fire and our ears stopped-up with all the things we need to be doing other than receiving God's word with our brothers and sisters.

Like my son preparing for his swim practice, we should prepare our lives so that we're ready for corporate worship. Be wise about how late you stay out or up the night before. Eat a good breakfast. Have all of your things together in one place so you're not hunting for your keys or Bible in the morning.

Prepare Your Heart

"Dinner starts at breakfast" was the advice I was given as a mom of young kids, and I needed it. If I didn't have a plan for dinner, I'd soon be overrun by the tyranny of the urgent. I'd run out of ingredients and either have to run out to the store or order food out (which wasn't in our budget and rarely as healthy). Even worse, sometimes I'd try rapidly to thaw some frozen ingredients! Even if I was able to pull off a fast and furious defrost, we all know rubbery chicken is hardly enjoyable. The moral of the story: Start preparing early.

Just as dinner starts at breakfast, our heart preparations for Sunday begin as early as Monday morning. As I noted earlier, if you happen to know what your pastor is preaching on Sunday, spend time reading that passage. Even better, study it with someone. If you're discipling another brother or sister, why not read through that passage and discuss it? You can even do this while you take a walk, make dinner, or meet for breakfast.

Parents, you can do this with your kids. Prepare them to hear God's word by reading the passage and discussing it with them. You can do that "formally" during a time of family worship or "informally" while driving to the next soccer practice.

If repetition is the mother of learning, why not read and reread God's word, so our hearts can better learn what God has to say to us?

I have a group of friends in our church who love to outline the passage for Sunday and see if it matches up to the sermon they hear. They look for how the passage connects to the gospel and try to anticipate how the preaching pastor will deliver the good news. When God's word is preached, they're ready to receive it! Few things are more edifying than preparing your heart to hear God's word.

Thoughts for Parents with Young Children

Currently, my husband and I are in what I like to call "the launching years" of parenting. Our home feels like the chaos of an international airport. We've got one independent adult in the air managed by air traffic control, two in college pulling away from the gate, and one still at home parked at the terminal. Juggling all the responsibilities of this season is challenging—it's also a little scary as we reflect on all the ways we both succeeded and failed to equip our kids for what lies ahead.

As Christian parents, God calls us to prepare our children to honor him in a sinful world. Deuteronomy 6:5–7 instructs us to teach our children to love the Lord our God with all their hearts, souls, and strength. That plays itself out in many ways, but one primary way is to instruct our kids not to neglect the weekly gathering of the saints.

My husband wasn't always a pastor. Like other Christian families, we struggled to get our family up on time, fed, dressed, and out the door for corporate worship without feeling (or looking!) haggard. It took a lot of planning and effort to prepare for worship well with four young children.

Over the years, we learned we needed to prepare everyone's clothes the night before and to plan meals for Sunday that weren't too complicated or too messy. Ultimately, learn to do what works for your family and your kids.

Remember, all your plans won't always run smoothly. You'll encounter mishaps and hiccups, but preparing your family for the Lord's Day will orient your family (and even your own heart) around God's word and his people.

A quick encouragement to fathers: Dads, don't leave all the prep work to your wife. Lead in preparing your family for the Sunday morning gathering.

Come Prepared to Serve

One way to prepare your heart for the weekly gathering is to pray beforehand for ways you can serve others. Look for a brother or sister who is in a challenging season, check in with them, and pray for them then and there. To serve others well, you have to arrive early enough to get into the building and checked into the nursery. Often, coming ready to serve involves simply being present and available to serve others.

Sometimes, Christians think they need a ministry assignment to effectively serve the church. But that's not true. Most of the ministry that takes place in a local church is informal and organic. There are countless ways to serve even without a formal "job," so keep your eyes and heart open, and pray that God would help you see how you can "love one another with brotherly affection" and "outdo one another in showing honor" (Rom. 12:10).

Enjoy a Meal with Others

There's something about food that draws people together in sweet intimacy. My husband and I love to open our home to our friends. We've also grown to love exercising hospitality with our church family after the Sunday morning service. We plan a meal with enough food for a few extra guests so we can get to know a visitor or encourage a member.

Of course, Sunday hospitality takes preparation and hard work. But whether you have a family, or you're a college student, or you're a single man in your fifties, exercising hospitality is a wonderful blessing.

Even more, exercising hospitality after the morning service fosters wonderful table discussions about the service and the sermon. Sunday lunch is a unique opportunity to put into action the words we have just sung, prayed, read, and heard minutes earlier.

Consider asking your guests if any of the song lyrics particularly encouraged them. Or consider saying something like, "As we eat, I'd love to hear one thing each of you found edifying in the sermon." Discussing and asking questions like this is one way for us to encourage each other and stir one another up toward love and good deeds (Heb. 10:24).

Maybe the idea of planning one more thing for Sunday feels overwhelming or even impossible. But consider if there are any creative ways you can get together with fellow members for "after-service meals."

Our church has groups of families who picnic in the park when the weather cooperates. Other friends of ours ask visitors and members to join them at local food court in the mall for lunch. Another group from our church eats out each Sunday, inviting visitors to join them and help them "see" the church interact as a family. If none of those options work, see if there's another single person or couple in the church who is already practicing hospitality and ask if you can join what they're doing. Offer to bring a salad or a simple side so you can serve them and learn from them.

Practicing hospitality on Sunday may be challenging, but it's one way we not only exalt the Lord together but edify one another and put the gospel on display for others to see.

When Sabbaths Have No End

The best way to prepare for the Sunday service is to know why we're meeting and what we're supposed to do when we gather. We train our hearts to sing like the Psalmist:

> For a day in your courts is better
> > than a thousand elsewhere.
> I would rather be a doorkeeper in the
> > house of my God
> > than dwell in the tents of wickedness.
> > (Ps. 84:10)

Why should we give so much time and attention to corporate worship? Because each gathering here on earth prepares us for the eternal gathering to come.

One day, the world as we know it will dissolve and God's people will be with their Savior in the new Jerusalem. Imagine that day! A congregation of God's people gathered around his throne forever. We will experience an eternity with God's people, exalting God and edifying one another. It will be an eternal Sabbath without end.[9]

Notes

1. Edmund P. Clowney, *The Church* (Lisle, IL: InterVarsity, 1995), 120.
2. Ligon Duncan, *Does God Care How We Worship* (Phillipsburg, NJ: P&R, 2020), 16.
3. It's sobering to think how most of these *died* for their wrong worship of the right God.
4. C. S. Lewis, *Letters to Malcolm: Chiefly on Prayer* (New York, NY: Harper One, 1992), 3.
5. Erin Wheeler, *The Good Portion, The Church: Delighting in the Doctrine of the Church* (Fearn, UK: Christian Focus, 2022), 96–97
6. Matt Merker, *Corporate Worship: How the Church Gathers as God's People* (Wheaton, IL: Crossway, 2021), 136.
7. For more thoughts on song selection and singing both songs of joy and sorrow, see Carl Trueman's essay, "What Can Miserable Christians Sing?" 9Marks, March 25, 2019, https://www.9marks.org. In it he states, "A diet of unremittingly jolly choruses and

hymns inevitably creates an unrealistic horizon of expectation which sees the normative Christian life as one long triumphalist street party—a theologically incorrect and a pastorally disastrous scenario in a world of broken individuals."

8. Matt Merker, *Corporate Worship: How the Church Gathers as God's People* (Wheaton, IL: Crossway, 2021), 150.

9. See lyrics to hymn, Joseph Bromehead, "Jerusalem, My Happy Home," 1776.

Scripture Index

Exodus
40:34 15

Leviticus
10:1–2 21–22

Numbers
9:15 15

Deuteronomy
6:5–7 37–38

1 Samuel
13:8–14 22

2 Samuel
6:3–7 22

1 Kings
8:1–11 15

Ezra
3:10–13 15

Psalms
84:10 42
121:1–2 33

Matthew
11:28–30 34
15:3 22

Luke
4:16 15
4:16–21 26

John
4:23–24 22

Acts
2:42 .... 25, 26
2:42–47 15
17:11 27
20:27 25

Scripture Index

Romans
12:10 39
15:6 31

1 Corinthians
11:27–30 22
12:12–31 30
12:20 16
14:24–25 18
14:40 26

Ephesians
5:18–20 31
6 34

Colossians
3:16 26

1 Timothy
2:8 26
4:13 25–26

Hebrews
10:24 41
10:24–25 34
12:28–29 22

Jude
20 15–16

9Marks
Building Healthy Churches

9Marks exists to equip church leaders with a biblical vision and practical resources for displaying God's glory to the nations through healthy churches.

To that end, we want to see churches characterized by these nine marks of health:

1. Expositional Preaching
2. Gospel Doctrine
3. A Biblical Understanding of Conversion and Evangelism
4. Biblical Church Membership
5. Biblical Church Discipline
6. A Biblical Concern for Discipleship and Growth
7. Biblical Church Leadership
8. A Biblical Understanding of the Practice of Prayer
9. A Biblical Understanding and Practice of Missions

Find all our Crossway titles and other resources at 9Marks.org.

IX 9Marks Church Questions

Providing ordinary Christians with sound and accessible biblical teaching by answering common questions about church life.

For more information, visit crossway.org.